Country Sampler's

*Christmas
Decorating Ideas*

Special thanks to: Paul and Sally Enstad, Dick and Sandy Hoffman, James and Bonnie Gauger, Joe and Pat Nemeth, Terry and Sue Ray, Jim and Charrie Colwell, Gary and Linda Smith, Chip and Sue Worthley, Steven and Lisa Lester, Robert and Julie Humphreys, Francis and Marilyn Hilditch, and Michael and Jennifer Reese for sharing their homes with us at Christmastime.

Country Sampler's Christmas Decorating Ideas
© 1987 by Sampler Publications, Inc.
All rights reserved

Photography: Dick Kaplan
Design: Mark D. Mazur
Room Stylist: Sue Worthley
Copy Editor: Laura Bersted

Published by Sampler Publications, Inc.
Country Sampler Books
Post Office Box 711
Glen Ellyn, IL 60138

ISBN 0–944493–01–7

Preface

Christmas is a special time that comes for a short time each year but lives in our hearts the whole year through. Because it is such a special time, extra care must be taken to ensure that everything in our homes is just right for the holiday.

The ambience of Christmas is evident in the homes we are about to visit. From treasures gathered at country shops and antique galleries, to those that have passed down for generations, to the ones we have handmade ourselves to pass to our children, these are the things that make each Christmas season something that is personal and special.

Through the following pages, you will witness how twelve families decorate their homes to make this season special for them. How they use greens, plants, ribbons, lights, and store-boughts to complement their keepsakes.

Keep this edition handy as a reference tool for decorating your home this Christmas. Find the decorating scenes that appeal to you or have similar special pieces you possess and use the ideas here to make your Christmas decorating even more fun than ever. Enjoy your tour through these lovely homes and we hope you find the ideas expressed here helpful for your Christmas decorating this year.

Table of Contents

The Enstad Home

Antique red and blue quilts find an appropriate place on the walls in the entry to the home of Paul, Sally, Erik, and Kelly Enstad. Throughout the home, navy and white are combined with antique cabinets, flea market treasures, homemade pillows, and primitive accessories. The openness of the floor plan is enhanced with primitives and provides an eclectic country atmosphere.

Ornaments of Scandinavian design, antique wooden cradles and chairs, and animals made of old quilts, highlight the Enstad tree at Christmas. On the wall, an old chair serves as a shelf to hold a candle.

In the dining room, a collection of prized crocks and pewter line the shelves of an antique open hutch.

A grapevine tree centers the quilt-topped dining room table.

Napkins finished with plaid bows are illuminated by candles at each place setting.

A primitive pie safe is a perfect place for storing extra dishes and tableware.

The navy and white kitchen is filled with collectibles and accented with red by the use of apples, bows, berries, and an old quilt used as a tablecloth. An antique tool box is a perfect home for country Christmas accents.

The Hoffman Home

Dick, Sandy, and Kip Hoffman welcome friends at Christmastime with cozy fires and remembrances of long ago. Their collections include antique toys, wooden containers, sleds, and primitive pine furniture collected at auctions, antique shows, and flea markets. A Shaker simplicity is enhanced by interesting groupings of collectibles.

Farm animals and bears are among the toys displayed on antique chairs and a New England trunk in a corner of Kip's room. A chimney cupboard houses books and toys. A wall-to-wall Shaker peg rack offers ample hanging space for antique buckets, sleds, and homespun children's wear.

An antique jelly cupboard houses a collection of tinware. The goose was made by Sandy's father. An antique sampler finds a special place on a shelf.

Toys, boxes, and bears are perched on an antique trunk. A favorite bear and his buddy hang from a Shaker peg rack.

The Gauger Home

Bonnie and Jim Gauger and their sons Jim and Jeff welcome you to their home filled with Santas, antique furniture, miniatures, and collections from Europe. A wreath displaying antique tin horns decorates the front door of their home.

Inside, antique wooden boxes from England find a home on the living room mantel. On the coffee table, a wooden pyramid from Germany welcomes guests.

An electrified Christmas dollhouse, made by Bonnie, depicts their family interests. A corner of the dining room houses bears, toys, and miniatures collected at flea markets and antique shows.

Antique Santas have a fitting place in an old pine dry sink. A blue and white kitchen is filled with flea market treasures. A walnut mug rack from England houses a collection of Santas and old pewter mugs.

The Nemeth Home

The country flavor begins at the front door to the home of Joe and Pat Nemeth and their children, Courtney, Matthew, Josh, Meghan and Amy, and continues throughout their home.

The angels lining the staircase in their entry were made by Pat. In the dining room, collections of mugs and "slip trailed" redware line the shelves of an antique hutch. Copper molds find an appropriate place on a wall above a 19th-century rocking horse.

Other collections include grey enamelware, antique Santas, and antique-shop treasures complemented by old red, putty, and blue.

An antique pine sled makes a perfect server for punch when guests arrive.

The tree, filled with flags and hearts, is for Amy, a newly adopted daughter who became a naturalized citizen at Christmastime.

A mini village with a feather tree and antique Santas is displayed atop an old 12-drawer chest. The hooked rug was made by Pat.

The Ray Home

In the home of Terry, Susan, and Eric Ray, antique bears, dolls, toys, and a barn made by Susan's father find an appropriate place under their tree.

Throughout the home, wreaths made from an assortment of natural materials from the Ray's own garden, are on display all year.

Susan's own artwork, combined with flea market and antique shop "finds" and creative dried arrangements, is among the collections that accent each room.

The Colwell Home

A "winter wonderland" is captured in the home of Jim and Charrie Colwell. Their antique Santas and shelves housing miniature villages are prominently displayed throughout the holiday season. Santas, bears, time-worn toys, and salesmen's samples find cozy niches under the tree.

The Smith Home

"Away in a Manger" is the holiday theme at the home of Gary and Linda Smith and their children, Ryan and Kurtis.

A wreath on the door, with a brass horn and music tied in a raffia bow, welcomes visitors.

Floorcloths and placemats in the kitchen, made and stenciled by Linda, are enhanced by their collection of pink depression glass. Stenciling throughout the house was also done by Linda.

In the foyer, the fabric manger scene on the lowboy was made by Linda. Angels, stars, and greenery adorn the staircase. The antique "courting table" on the landing has been in the family for generations.

The Worthley Home

The colors of old red and navy, complemented by country primitives and flea market treasures can be found throughout the home of Chip, Sue, Amy, Emily and Mark Worthley.

Their dog, Brandy, relaxes next to a tree filled with the children's own ornaments collected each year.

Stenciling throughout the home was done by Sue.

In the kitchen an old chicken hatcher, bearing the original red stain, houses breadboards and antique crockery. The mini Santas on the tree were made by Sue.

Baskets, buckets, and primitive cupboards adorn the family room. On the coffee table an antique tool box is filled with candles, greens and cinnamon sticks.

The Lester Home

The colors of cranberry and blue, highlighted by Christmas greens and accented with antiques, can be seen throughout the home of Steve, Lisa, Katie and Martha Lester.

In the family room, a "bear" tree, accented with Katie's and Martha's own collection, is the center of attention.

In the den, homemade bread, a gift for neighbors, is ready for delivery.

The Humphreys Home

The 19th-century Victorian home of Robert, Julie, Robert, and Amy Humphreys combines the intense colors of deep rose, black, and museum white throughout, with an authentic Victorian culture.

Leaded stained glass windows, original to the house, enhance the turret in the foyer. An open staircase to the third floor boasts hand-turned spindles and a handcarved newel post.

The Hilditch Home

Shaker simplicity, wooden whirligigs, and antique toys and bears highlight the home of Francis and Marilyn Hilditch. A tree of baby's breath, candles, plaid bows, and apples welcomes guests during the holidays.

Inside, the owners' talents are evident in the handcarved shorebirds and hand-hooked rugs displayed throughout the home. The stencils were designed and cut by Marilyn who also did all the detailing.

The Reese Home

The coziness of this New England-style farmhouse of Michael, Jennifer, Becky and Sarah Reese, lends a warm welcome to guests during the holidays.

Teddies of antique quilts, an old Union churn with original stenciling, crocks, and packages, huddle on the porch where the family cat, Sneakers, waits for guests.

Inside, wood-peg floors, cherry and pine cupboards, stenciling, and the colors of blue and dusty rose combine to give this new home a true country flavor.